Polymer

Creative Techniques and Inspired Designs

Jerry Dylan
copyright@2024

Table of Content

CHAPTER 1

    Introduction to Polymer Clay

    What is Polymer Clay?

    History

CHAPTER 2

    Getting Started with Polymer Clay

    Essential Tools and Materials

    Baking Instructions for Polymer Clay

    Safety Precautions

CHAPTER 3

    Essential Techniques

    Basic Techniques for Working with Polymer Clay

    Creating Beads with Polymer Clay

CHAPTER 4

    Making Pendants and Charms with Polymer Clay

    Incorporating Metal Findings and Wirework into Polymer Clay Jewelry

CHAPTER 5

    Advanced Techniques

    Adding Finishing Touches

CHAPTER 6

    Beginner Projects

    Simple Polymer Clay Earrings

    Clay Bead Bracelet

- Keychain or Bag Charm
- Polymer Clay Pendant Necklace
- Polymer Clay Magnets
- Polymer Clay Coasters

CHAPTER 7
- Intermediate Projects
- Polymer Clay Mosaic Tray
- Polymer Clay Flower Vase
- Polymer Clay Pendant with Faux Gemstone Inlay
- Polymer Clay Picture Frame

CHAPTER 8
- Advanced Projects
- Polymer Clay Millefiori Bowl
- Polymer Clay Sculpture
- Polymer Clay Filigree Earrings
- Polymer Clay Wall Art
- Polymer Clay Kaleidoscope Cane
- Polymer Clay Mosaic Wall Art

CHAPTER 9
- Troubleshooting and Tips
- General Tips

CONCLUSION

CHAPTER 1
Introduction to Polymer Clay

What is Polymer Clay?

Polymer clay is a type of modeling clay that remains pliable until cured in an oven. It's composed of a polyvinyl chloride (PVC) base, along with plasticizers and pigments. Once cured, usually at relatively low temperatures (around 275°F or 130°C), it becomes hard and durable, making it ideal for crafting various items, including jewelry, figurines, and decorative objects.

Polymer clay comes in a wide range of colors and can be manipulated, shaped, and textured to create intricate designs. It's popular among artists and crafters due to its versatility and ability to mimic other materials like stone, metal, or ceramic.

History

Polymer clay has an interesting history that dates back to the mid-20th century.

Origin: Polymer clay was first developed in Germany during the 1930s as a material for doll-making. However, its potential for other applications was not fully realized until later.

Commercialization: In the 1960s, a company called Eberhard Faber began marketing a type of polymer clay under the brand name "Fimo" in Germany. Fimo quickly gained popularity among hobbyists and artists for its versatility and ease of use.

Expansion: In the 1970s, Fimo was introduced to the United States and other parts of the world, further expanding its popularity. Other brands of polymer clay, such as Sculpey and Kato Polyclay, also emerged during this time.

Artistic Evolution: Throughout the 1980s and 1990s, polymer clay artists began experimenting with new techniques and applications, pushing the boundaries of what could be achieved with the material. Polymer clay gained recognition as a legitimate medium for creating fine art and jewelry.

Online Communities: With the advent of the internet, online communities and forums dedicated to polymer clay emerged, allowing artists to share techniques, tutorials, and inspiration with a global audience.

Modern Trends: Today, polymer clay continues to be a popular medium for artists and crafters around the world. Its versatility, affordability, and accessibility make it an ideal choice for creating everything from jewelry and figurines to home decor and mixed media art.

CHAPTER 2
Getting Started with Polymer Clay

Essential Tools and Materials

Polymer Clay: Choose from a variety of brands and colors to suit your project.

Work Surface: A smooth, non-porous surface such as ceramic tile, glass, or acrylic sheet to work on.

Cutting Tools: Sharp blades or craft knives for cutting clay and creating clean edges.

Rolling Pin or Pasta Machine: For rolling out clay to a uniform thickness.

Texture Tools: Stamps, texture sheets, or household items like fabric, leaves, and buttons for adding texture to the clay.

Sculpting Tools: Tools for shaping, carving, and detailing clay, such as ball styluses, clay shapers, and dental tools.

Baking Surface: A baking sheet or tile to place your clay creations on while baking.

Oven: A household oven or dedicated toaster oven for curing polymer clay according to manufacturer's instructions.

Protective Gear: Gloves, dust mask, and safety glasses for protection when working with clay and during sanding.

Sanding Tools: Sandpaper or sanding sponges in various grits for sanding rough edges and achieving a smooth finish.

Finishing Materials: Acrylic varnish, resin, or liquid clay for sealing and adding a glossy or matte finish to your creations.

Jewelry Findings: Jump rings, earring hooks, necklace chains, and clasps for assembling finished jewelry pieces.

Storage Containers: Containers or organizers for storing clay, tools, and finished jewelry pieces.

Baking Instructions for Polymer Clay
Preheat the Oven:

Preheat your oven to the temperature recommended by the polymer clay manufacturer. Most polymer clays cure at around 265-275°F (130-135°C).

Prepare the Baking Surface:

Place your clay pieces on a non-stick surface, such as a ceramic tile, a piece of parchment paper, or an aluminum foil-covered baking sheet. Avoid using glass or any surface that retains heat for too long after baking, as this can lead to over-baking.

Bake According to Thickness:

The general rule is to bake polymer clay for 30 minutes per 1/4 inch (6 mm) of thickness. For example, if your piece is 1/2 inch (12 mm) thick, it should be baked for 60 minutes. For optimal results, always follow the manufacturer's instructions.

Monitor the Temperature:

Use an oven thermometer to ensure the temperature remains consistent and accurate throughout the baking process. Oven temperatures can vary, and polymer clay can scorch if the temperature is too high.

Cool Down:

After baking, let the pieces cool completely on the baking surface before handling. They will harden as they cool.

Safety Precautions

Ventilation:

Ensure your workspace is well-ventilated. Polymer clay can release fumes when baking, which, although generally considered non-toxic, should not be inhaled in large quantities.

Dedicated Oven:

If possible, use a dedicated toaster oven for baking polymer clay to avoid any contamination with food. If you use your kitchen oven, ensure it's thoroughly cleaned after each use.

Avoid Over-baking:

Over-baking can cause the clay to scorch or produce more fumes. Always follow the recommended baking times and temperatures.

Proper Handling:

Wash your hands before and after handling polymer clay to avoid contamination and potential skin irritation. Some people may be sensitive to the plasticizers in the clay.

Making Basic Shapes

Learning to create basic shapes is crucial for more complex projects.

Beads: Roll clay into small balls, pierce them with a needle or toothpick, and bake.

Pendants: Cut or sculpt flat shapes from clay sheets, adding holes for stringing before baking.

Layering

Layering involves adding pieces of clay on top of one another to create designs.

Canes: Create cylindrical patterns by layering different colors and shapes of clay, which can then be sliced to reveal intricate designs.

Stacking: Place thin layers of clay on top of each other, pressing gently to ensure they adhere well before baking.

Marbling

Marbling combines colors to create a swirled effect.

Cutting: Use craft knives, cookie cutters, or clay blades to cut shapes out of flattened clay.

Blending Colors

Blending colors can create gradients, marbled effects, and unique shades.

Mixing: Combine two or more colors by conditioning them together until you achieve the desired blend.

Skinner Blend: Create a gradient by laying two different colors of clay next to each other, folding them, and running them through a pasta machine repeatedly.

Texturing

Adding texture can give your clay pieces a more interesting surface.

Tools: Use household items like lace, leaves, sandpaper, or dedicated texture sheets to press patterns into the clay.

Impressing: Press objects like buttons, stamps, or sculpting tools into the clay to create impressions.

CHAPTER 3
Essential Techniques

Basic Techniques for Working with Polymer Clay

Conditioning

Conditioning polymer clay is essential to make it pliable and eliminate air bubbles.

Kneading by Hand: Warm up the clay by rolling and kneading it in your hands until it becomes soft and pliable.

Pasta Machine: Run the clay through a pasta machine several times, folding it in half and rotating it between passes, until the clay is smooth and flexible.

Shaping

Shaping techniques form the foundation of your polymer clay creations.

Rolling: Use a rolling pin or acrylic roller to flatten clay to the desired thickness.

Protective Gear:

Use gloves if you have sensitive skin, and consider wearing a dust mask when sanding cured clay to avoid inhaling fine particles.

Keep Away from Food:

Do not use kitchen utensils or tools that will be used for food preparation with polymer clay. Have a separate set of tools specifically for your clay work.

Storage:

Store polymer clay in a cool, dry place, keeping it away from direct sunlight and heat sources. Keep it in airtight containers to prevent it from becoming brittle or drying out.

Twisting: Twist two or more colors of clay together, then fold and twist again until you achieve the desired pattern.

Rolling: Roll the twisted clay into a log and slice it to reveal the marbled interior.

Piercing and Drilling

Creating holes in your clay pieces allows for stringing and assembling jewelry.

Pre-baking: Use needles, toothpicks, or specialized clay tools to pierce holes before baking.

Post-baking: Use a small hand drill to make precise holes in baked clay pieces.

Smoothing and Finishing

Ensuring a smooth finish enhances the look of your final piece.

Smoothing: Use wet wipes or your fingertips to gently smooth the surface before baking.

Sanding: After baking, sand your pieces with fine-grit sandpaper to remove imperfections.

Creating Beads with Polymer Clay

Basic Round Beads

Materials and Tools:

- Polymer clay
- Needle or toothpick
- Clay blade or craft knife
- Sandpaper (optional)

Steps:

Condition the Clay: Knead and soften the clay until it's pliable.

Forming Beads: Pinch off small pieces of clay and roll them between your palms to form round beads.

Piercing Holes: Insert a needle or toothpick through the center of each bead to create a hole for stringing. Rotate the needle to ensure the hole is smooth and even.

Baking: Place the beads on a baking sheet and bake according to the manufacturer's instructions. Be sure to place the beads on a bead rack or suspend them on a needle to prevent flat spots.

Sanding and Finishing: After baking, sand the beads lightly with fine-grit sandpaper if needed for a smoother finish.

Tube Beads

Materials and Tools:

- Polymer clay
- Needle or skewer
- Rolling pin
- Clay blade or craft knife

Steps:

Condition the Clay: Soften the clay by kneading it thoroughly.

Rolling Clay: Roll out the clay to the desired thickness using a rolling pin.

Cutting Shapes: Cut the flattened clay into rectangular strips.

Forming Tubes: Wrap the strips around a needle or skewer to form tube-shaped beads. Ensure the ends meet and blend them together to secure.

Piercing Holes: Keep the needle or skewer in place to maintain the hole during baking.

Baking: Bake the beads while still on the needle or skewer to ensure the holes stay intact.

Finishing: Sand the edges if necessary after baking for a clean finish.

Textured Beads

Materials and Tools:

- Polymer clay
- Texture tools (stamps, texture sheets, household items)
- Needle or toothpick

Steps:

Condition the Clay: Prepare the clay by kneading it until it's soft.

Forming Beads: Shape the clay into round or other desired shapes.

Adding Texture: Press texture tools into the surface of the beads to create patterns. Roll the beads gently to ensure the texture is evenly applied.

Piercing Holes: Use a needle or toothpick to create holes for stringing.

Baking: Place the beads on a baking sheet and bake according to the clay manufacturer's instructions.

Finishing: If needed, sand lightly and apply a sealer or varnish to enhance the texture.

Cane Beads

Materials and Tools:

- Polymer clay in multiple colors
- Rolling pin or pasta machine
- Clay blade or craft knife
- Needle or toothpick

Steps:

Condition the Clay: Soften different colors of clay by kneading.

Creating Canes: Form a cane by layering and rolling different colors of clay together into a log. Shape and reduce the cane to the desired size.

Cutting Slices: Slice the cane into thin pieces using a sharp blade.

Forming Beads: Roll the cane slices into beads or apply them to the surface of round beads.

Piercing Holes: Create holes for stringing with a needle or toothpick.

Baking: Bake the beads according to the clay's instructions.

Finishing: Sand and buff the beads if necessary to bring out the colors and patterns.

Marbled Beads

Materials and Tools:

- Polymer clay in different colors
- Rolling pin
- Needle or toothpick

Steps:

Condition the Clay: Knead the different colors of clay separately.

Mixing Colors: Roll and twist the colors together to create a marbled effect, but do not over-mix.

Forming Beads: Shape the marbled clay into beads by rolling between your palms.

Piercing Holes: Use a needle or toothpick to create holes for stringing.

Baking: Place the beads on a baking sheet and bake according to the manufacturer's instructions.

Finishing: Sand and buff the beads after baking to enhance the marbled effect.

CHAPTER 4
Making Pendants and Charms with Polymer Clay

Basic Flat Pendants

Materials and Tools:

- Polymer clay
- Rolling pin or acrylic roller
- Cookie cutters or clay cutters
- Needle or skewer
- Sandpaper (optional)

Steps:

Condition the Clay: Knead the clay until it is soft and pliable.

Rolling Out Clay: Roll the clay to an even thickness, typically around 1/8 inch (3 mm).

Cutting Shapes: Use cookie cutters or clay cutters to cut out the desired shapes for your pendants.

Creating Holes: Use a needle or skewer to make holes for hanging the pendants. Ensure the holes are large enough to accommodate jump rings or cords.

Baking: Place the pendants on a baking sheet and bake according to the clay manufacturer's instructions.

Sanding and Finishing: After baking, sand the edges if necessary for a smooth finish. Apply a varnish or sealer if desired.

Textured Pendants

Materials and Tools:

- Polymer clay
- Texture sheets or household items (e.g., lace, leaves)
- Rolling pin
- Needle or skewer

Steps:

Condition the Clay: Prepare the clay by kneading it until it's soft.

Rolling Out Clay: Roll the clay to an even thickness.

Adding Texture: Press texture sheets or household items into the clay to create patterns.

Cutting Shapes: Use cutters to cut out shapes from the textured clay.

Creating Holes: Make holes for hanging the pendants with a needle or skewer.

Baking: Bake the pendants according to the manufacturer's instructions.

Finishing: Sand the edges if needed and apply a finish to enhance the texture.

Layered Pendants

Materials and Tools:

- Polymer clay in different colors
- Rolling pin
- Clay blade or craft knife
- Needle or skewer

Steps:

Condition the Clay: Knead each color of clay until soft.

Rolling Out Layers: Roll out each color into thin sheets.

Layering: Stack the sheets on top of each other, pressing gently to ensure they adhere.

Cutting Shapes: Use cutters to cut out shapes from the layered clay.

Creating Holes: Make holes for hanging the pendants with a needle or skewer.

Baking: Bake the pendants as per the manufacturer's instructions.

Finishing: Sand the edges and apply a finish if desired.

Sculpted Charms

Materials and Tools:

- Polymer clay
- Sculpting tools (e.g., ball stylus, needle tools)
- Needle or skewer

Steps:

Condition the Clay: Knead the clay until it is soft.

Sculpting: Use your hands and sculpting tools to shape the clay into miniatures or specific designs (e.g., animals, flowers, symbols).

Creating Holes: Use a needle or skewer to make holes for hanging.

Baking: Place the charms on a baking sheet and bake according to the clay manufacturer's instructions.

Finishing: Sand and smooth any rough edges after baking. Apply a varnish or sealer if desired.

Mixed Media Pendants

Materials and Tools:

- Polymer clay
- Additional materials (e.g., metal findings, beads, mica powders)
- Rolling pin
- Needle or skewer

Steps:

Condition the Clay: Knead the clay until soft.

Rolling Out Clay: Roll the clay to the desired thickness.

Embedding Materials: Press beads, metal findings, or other materials into the clay.

Adding Color: Apply mica powders or other surface treatments if desired.

Cutting Shapes: Use cutters to cut out the shapes for your pendants.

Creating Holes: Make holes for hanging the pendants.

Baking: Bake the pendants according to the manufacturer's instructions.

Finishing: Apply any additional finishes or sealers as needed.

Incorporating Metal Findings and Wirework into Polymer Clay Jewelry

Embedding Eye Pins or Headpins

Materials and Tools:

- Polymer clay
- Eye pins or headpins
- Rolling pin
- Clay blade or craft knife
- Needle or skewer

Steps:

Condition the Clay: Knead the clay until soft and pliable.

Rolling Out Clay: Roll the clay to the desired thickness.

Cutting Shapes: Use a clay blade or craft knife to cut out shapes for your jewelry pieces.

Embedding Eye Pins/Headpins: Insert eye pins or headpins into the clay pieces, ensuring they are securely embedded.

Baking: Bake the clay according to the manufacturer's instructions, making sure not to overheat the metal findings.

Finishing: After baking, allow the clay to cool completely before removing from the oven. Ensure the metal findings are firmly embedded.

Creating Bezels for Cabochons

Materials and Tools:

- Polymer clay
- Cabochons
- Metal bezel findings
- Rolling pin
- Clay blade or craft knife
- Sandpaper (optional)

Steps:

Condition the Clay: Knead the clay until soft and pliable.

Rolling Out Clay: Roll the clay to the desired thickness.

Cutting Shapes: Use a clay blade or craft knife to cut out a shape slightly larger than your cabochon.

Pressing in Cabochon: Press the cabochon firmly into the clay to create an impression.

Adding Metal Bezel: Place the metal bezel finding on top of the clay, ensuring it fits snugly around the cabochon impression.

Baking: Bake the clay according to the manufacturer's instructions, taking care not to overheat the metal bezel finding.

Finishing: After baking, allow the clay to cool completely before removing from the oven. Optionally, sand any rough edges and polish the metal bezel for a professional finish.

Wire Wrapping

Materials and Tools:

- Polymer clay
- Jewelry wire (e.g., copper, silver, gold)
- Wire cutters

- Round-nose pliers
- Needle or skewer

Steps:

Condition the Clay: Knead the clay until soft and pliable.

Rolling Out Clay: Roll the clay to the desired thickness.

Cutting Shapes: Use a clay blade or craft knife to cut out shapes for your jewelry pieces.

Creating Holes: Make holes for hanging the pieces using a needle or skewer.

Wire Wrapping: Cut a length of jewelry wire and create a loop using round-nose pliers. Thread the wire through the hole in the clay piece and wrap it securely around the loop.

Baking: Bake the clay according to the manufacturer's instructions, ensuring the wire is securely attached.

Finishing: After baking, allow the clay to cool completely before removing from the oven. Optionally, polish the wire for a shiny finish.

Attaching Jump Rings and Clasps

Materials and Tools:

- Polymer clay
- Jump rings
- Clasps
- Needle or skewer
- Pliers (optional)

Steps:

Condition the Clay: Knead the clay until soft and pliable.

Rolling Out Clay: Roll the clay to the desired thickness.

Cutting Shapes: Use a clay blade or craft knife to cut out shapes for your jewelry pieces.

Creating Holes: Make holes for attaching jump rings and clasps using a needle or skewer.

Attaching Jump Rings: Open a jump ring using pliers (if needed), thread it through the hole in the clay piece, and close it securely.

Attaching Clasps: Attach clasps to the ends of chains or cords using jump rings in the same manner.

Baking: Bake the clay according to the manufacturer's instructions, ensuring the jump rings and clasps are securely attached.

Finishing: After baking, allow the clay to cool completely before removing from the oven. Optionally, polish metal findings for a professional finish.

CHAPTER 5
Advanced Techniques

Millefiori Canes

Millefiori canes involve creating intricate patterns or images within a cylindrical clay log, which can then be sliced to reveal the design. This technique is reminiscent of glasswork and can yield stunning results.

Materials and Tools:

- Polymer clay in various colors
- Rolling pin or pasta machine
- Blade or craft knife
- Work surface

Steps:

Prepare the Clay: Condition each color of clay by kneading until soft and pliable.

Create a Base Color: Choose a base color for your cane and roll it into a thick log.

Add Additional Colors: Roll out thin sheets of different colored clays and layer them onto the base color. Stack the colors to create a pattern or image.

Roll into a Log: Carefully roll the layered clay into a tight log, ensuring the layers stick together without air pockets.

Reduce the Log: Gently roll the log on your work surface to elongate it and reduce its diameter. Continue rolling until the log is the desired size.

Slice the Cane: Using a sharp blade or craft knife, carefully slice the cane into thin discs. Each slice will reveal a cross-section of the layered pattern.

Arrange and Bake: Arrange the cane slices onto a baking sheet and bake according to the manufacturer's instructions. Be mindful not to distort the shape of the slices during handling.

Cool and Finish: Allow the slices to cool completely before handling. Sand any rough edges if necessary, and incorporate them into your jewelry designs.

Surface Techniques: Marbling and Texturing

Surface techniques involve manipulating the surface of the clay to create texture, patterns, and visual interest.

Materials and Tools:

- Polymer clay in various colors
- Texture tools (stamps, texture sheets, household items)
- Rolling pin
- Blade or craft knife
- Work surface

Steps:

Prepare the Clay: Condition each color of clay by kneading until soft and pliable.

Marbling:

Roll out each color of clay into thin sheets.

Stack the sheets on top of each other, alternating colors.

Fold the stacked sheets in half and roll them into a log.

Twist and fold the log several times to create a marbled effect.

Roll out the marbled clay to the desired thickness and use it in your jewelry designs.

Texturing:

Roll out a sheet of clay to your desired thickness.

Press texture tools, stamps, or household items into the clay to create patterns and texture.

Experiment with different textures and combinations to achieve unique effects.

Use the textured clay as a base for your jewelry pieces or incorporate it into layered designs.

Bake and Finish:

Bake the clay as directed by the manufacturer's instructions.

Once cooled, sand any rough edges if necessary and incorporate the marbled or textured clay into your jewelry designs.

Sculpting Figurines

Sculpting figurines involves shaping polymer clay into three-dimensional forms, such as animals, people, or fantastical creatures.

Materials and Tools:

- Polymer clay in various colors
- Sculpting tools (ball stylus, needle tools)
- Work surface

Steps:

Plan Your Design: Visualize the figurine you want to create and gather reference images for inspiration.

Prepare the Clay: Condition each color of clay by kneading until soft and pliable.

Build Armature (Optional): If creating a large or complex figurine, consider creating an armature using wire or aluminum foil to provide structure and support.

Basic Shapes: Begin by forming the basic shapes of the figurine's body parts (e.g., head, torso, limbs) using balls, logs, or coils of clay.

Refine Details: Use sculpting tools to add details such as facial features, clothing, and texture. Work gradually, starting with larger details and refining them as you progress.

Assemble Parts: Attach the various components of the figurine together, blending seams carefully to create a seamless appearance.

Bake: Place the figurine on a baking sheet and bake according to the manufacturer's instructions. Be careful not to distort the shape of the figurine during handling.

Cool and Finish: Allow the figurine to cool completely before handling. Sand any rough edges if necessary, and paint or seal the figurine to enhance its appearance.

Surface Inlays

Surface inlays involve embedding materials into the surface of polymer clay to create intricate designs and patterns.

Materials and Tools:

- Polymer clay
- Inlay materials (e.g., metal leaf, crushed stones, mica powders)
- Texture tools (stamps, texture sheets)
- Rolling pin
- Blade or craft knife
- Work surface

Steps:

Prepare the Clay: Condition the clay by kneading until soft and pliable.

Roll Out Clay: Roll out a sheet of clay to the desired thickness on a clean work surface.

Create Base Design: Use texture tools, stamps, or other objects to create a base design on the clay surface.

Prepare Inlay Materials: Crush or cut your chosen inlay materials into small pieces or shapes.

Apply Inlay Materials: Press the inlay materials into the clay surface within the designated areas of the base design. You can arrange them randomly or design specific patterns.

Roll Over: Gently roll over the surface with a rolling pin to ensure the inlay materials are embedded securely into the clay.

Trim Excess: Use a blade or craft knife to trim away any excess clay around the edges of the design.

Bake: Place the clay on a baking sheet and bake according to the manufacturer's instructions.

Cool and Finish: Allow the clay to cool completely before handling. Sand any rough edges if necessary, and apply a finish or sealant to enhance the appearance of the inlay design.

Adding Finishing Touches

Adding finishing touches to polymer clay jewelry pieces can elevate their appearance and make them look more polished and professional.

Sanding and Buffing

After baking, use fine-grit sandpaper or sanding sponges to smooth any rough edges or surfaces on your clay pieces.

Gradually increase the grit size for a smoother finish.

Buff the surface with a soft cloth or a buffing wheel attachment on a rotary tool to achieve a glossy shine.

Painting and Coloring

Use acrylic paints or alcohol inks to add color to your polymer clay pieces.

Apply paint or ink with a fine brush or sponge applicator, allowing it to dry completely before sealing with a clear varnish or resin.

Adding Texture and Detail

Use metallic powders or mica powders to highlight texture and details on your clay pieces.

Apply the powders with a soft brush or sponge applicator, then buff gently to enhance the shine.

Embedding Gemstones or Beads

Press small gemstones, beads, or other embellishments into the surface of your clay pieces before baking.

Ensure the embellishments are securely embedded and won't come loose during baking or wear.

Surface Treatments

Experiment with surface treatments such as antiquing or patina effects to give your clay pieces a vintage or aged appearance.

Apply the treatment with a soft brush or sponge, then wipe away excess with a clean cloth or paper towel.

Sealing and Varnishing

Apply a clear varnish or resin to your polymer clay pieces to protect them from wear and tear and give them a glossy finish.

Follow the manufacturer's instructions for the varnish or resin you choose, and allow it to dry completely before handling.

Adding Metal Findings

Attach metal findings such as jump rings, clasps, or earring hooks to your clay pieces using jewelry glue or by embedding them before baking.

Ensure the metal findings are securely attached and won't come loose during wear.

Personalizing with Stamping or Engraving

Stamp or engrave designs, patterns, or personal messages onto your clay pieces using metal stamps or engraving tools.

Press the stamps or tools firmly into the clay surface before baking, then bake according to the clay manufacturer's instructions.

CHAPTER 6
Beginner Projects

Simple Polymer Clay Earrings

Materials Needed:

- Polymer clay (2 or more colors)
- Earring hooks or posts
- Jump rings (optional)
- Rolling pin or pasta machine
- Clay blade or craft knife
- Needle or toothpick
- Baking sheet and oven

Steps:

Condition the Clay: Knead the polymer clay until it's soft and pliable.

Roll Out Clay: Roll out the clay to your desired thickness using a rolling pin or pasta machine.

Cut Shapes: Use a clay blade or craft knife to cut out shapes for your earrings. You can make simple geometric shapes like circles, squares, or triangles.

Poke Holes: Use a needle or toothpick to poke a hole at the top of each shape for attaching earring hooks.

Add Texture or Design (optional): Use stamps, texture sheets, or other tools to add texture or designs to the surface of your earrings.

Bake: Place the earrings on a baking sheet and bake according to the clay manufacturer's instructions.

Attach Earring Hooks: Once the earrings have cooled, attach earring hooks or posts to the holes you made earlier. You can also add jump rings for extra flair.

Finishing Touches: Sand any rough edges if necessary and apply a gloss varnish for a shiny finish (optional).

Clay Bead Bracelet

Materials Needed:

- Polymer clay (multiple colors)
- Stretch cord or jewelry wire
- Clay roller or pasta machine
- Clay cutter or craft knife
- Baking sheet and oven

Steps:

Condition the Clay: Knead the polymer clay until it's soft and pliable.

Roll Out Clay: Roll out each color of clay to your desired thickness using a clay roller or pasta machine.

Cut Beads: Use a clay cutter or craft knife to cut out beads from the rolled-out clay.

You can make beads in various shapes and sizes.

Create Patterns (optional): Layer different colors of clay, twist them together, or add texture to create patterns on the beads.

Poke Holes: Use a needle or toothpick to poke a hole through the center of each bead for stringing.

Bake: Place the beads on a baking sheet and bake according to the clay manufacturer's instructions.

String Beads: Once the beads have cooled, string them onto stretch cord or jewelry wire in your desired pattern.

Secure and Finish: Tie a knot at the ends of the cord or wire to secure the beads in place. Trim any excess cord or wire. Optionally, add a drop of glue to the knots for extra security.

Keychain or Bag Charm

Materials Needed:

- Polymer clay (1 or more colors)
- Keychain ring or lobster clasp
- Rolling pin or pasta machine
- Clay blade or craft knife
- Needle or toothpick
- Baking sheet and oven

Steps:

Condition the Clay: Knead the polymer clay until it's soft and pliable.

Roll Out Clay: Roll out the clay to your desired thickness using a rolling pin or pasta machine.

Cut Shape: Use a clay blade or craft knife to cut out a shape for your keychain or bag charm. You can make simple shapes like hearts, stars, or animals.

Add Texture or Design (optional): Use stamps, texture sheets, or other tools to add texture or designs to the surface of your charm.

Poke Hole: Use a needle or toothpick to poke a hole at the top of the charm for attaching the keychain ring or lobster clasp.

Bake: Place the charm on a baking sheet and bake according to the clay manufacturer's instructions.

Attach Keychain Ring or Lobster Clasp: Once the charm has cooled, attach a keychain ring or lobster clasp to the hole you made earlier.

Finishing Touches: Sand any rough edges if necessary and apply a gloss varnish for a shiny finish (optional).

Polymer Clay Pendant Necklace

Materials Needed:

- Polymer clay (1 or more colors)
- Necklace chain or cord
- Rolling pin or pasta machine
- Clay blade or craft knife
- Needle or toothpick
- Baking sheet and oven

Steps:

Condition the Clay: Knead the polymer clay until it's soft and pliable.

Roll Out Clay: Roll out the clay to your desired thickness using a rolling pin or pasta machine.

Cut Shape: Use a clay blade or craft knife to cut out a shape for your pendant. You can make simple shapes like circles, ovals, or rectangles.

Add Texture or Design (optional): Use stamps, texture sheets, or other tools to add texture or designs to the surface of your pendant.

Poke Hole: Use a needle or toothpick to poke a hole at the top of the pendant for stringing onto the necklace chain or cord.

Bake: Place the pendant on a baking sheet and bake according to the clay manufacturer's instructions.

String Pendant: Once the pendant has cooled, string it onto a necklace chain or cord.

Finishing Touches: Add a clasp or closure to the necklace chain or cord if needed. Sand any rough edges if necessary and apply a gloss varnish for a shiny finish (optional).

Polymer Clay Magnets

Materials Needed:

- Polymer clay (various colors)
- Magnet discs or strips
- Rolling pin or pasta machine
- Cookie cutters or clay cutters
- Clay blade or craft knife
- Baking sheet and oven

Steps:

Condition the Clay: Knead the polymer clay until it's soft and pliable.

Roll Out Clay: Roll out the clay to your desired thickness using a rolling pin or pasta machine.

Cut Shapes: Use cookie cutters or clay cutters to cut out shapes for your magnets. You can make simple shapes like hearts, stars, or animals.

Add Texture or Design (optional): Use stamps, texture sheets, or other tools to add texture or designs to the surface of your magnets.

Attach Magnets: Press a magnet disc or strip onto the back of each clay shape.

Bake: Place the magnets on a baking sheet and bake according to the clay manufacturer's instructions.

Cool and Finish: Allow the magnets to cool completely before handling. Optionally, sand any rough edges if necessary and apply a gloss varnish for a shiny finish.

Polymer Clay Coasters

Materials Needed:

- Polymer clay (various colors)

- Rolling pin or pasta machine
- Coaster mold or round object for shaping
- Clay blade or craft knife
- Baking sheet and oven

Steps:

Condition the Clay: Knead the polymer clay until it's soft and pliable.

Roll Out Clay: Roll out the clay to your desired thickness using a rolling pin or pasta machine.

Cut Shapes: Use a clay blade or craft knife to cut out circles or squares for your coasters. You can also use a coaster mold for uniform shapes.

Add Texture or Design (optional): Use stamps, texture sheets, or other tools to add texture or designs to the surface of your coasters.

Bake: Place the coasters on a baking sheet and bake according to the clay manufacturer's instructions.

Cool and Finish: Allow the coasters to cool completely before handling. Optionally, sand any rough edges if necessary and apply a gloss varnish for a shiny finish.

CHAPTER 7
Intermediate Projects

Polymer Clay Mosaic Tray

Materials Needed:

- Polymer clay (various colors)
- Wooden or ceramic tray
- Rolling pin or pasta machine
- Clay blade or craft knife
- Liquid polymer clay or translucent liquid clay
- Baking sheet and oven
- Sandpaper (optional)

Steps:

Prepare the Base: Clean and sand the surface of the tray if necessary. Roll out a thin sheet of polymer clay and cover the base of the tray with it, smoothing out any air bubbles or wrinkles.

Create Mosaic Tiles: Roll out sheets of polymer clay in various colors. Use a clay blade or craft knife to cut the sheets into small, geometric shapes like squares, triangles, or rectangles. You can also use clay cutters for uniform shapes.

Arrange Tiles: Arrange the clay tiles on the base of the tray in a mosaic pattern. Experiment with different colors and shapes to create visually interesting designs.

Secure Tiles: Once you're satisfied with the arrangement, lightly press each clay tile onto the base to adhere them. You can also use a small amount of liquid polymer clay or translucent liquid clay to help secure the tiles in place.

Fill Gaps: Use smaller pieces of clay to fill in any gaps between the tiles, ensuring a smooth and cohesive surface.

Bake: Place the tray on a baking sheet and bake according to the polymer clay manufacturer's instructions. Let the tray cool completely before handling.

Finish: Optionally, sand the edges of the tray for a smoother finish. Apply a thin coat of clear varnish or resin to seal and protect the surface of the tray.

Polymer Clay Flower Vase

Materials Needed:

- Polymer clay (various colors)
- Glass or ceramic vase
- Rolling pin or pasta machine
- Clay blade or craft knife
- Liquid polymer clay or translucent liquid clay
- Baking sheet and oven
- Sculpting tools (optional)

Steps:

Prepare the Base: Clean the surface of the vase and roll out a thin sheet of polymer clay. Cover the vase with the clay sheet, smoothing out any air bubbles or wrinkles.

Create Flower Components: Roll out sheets of polymer clay in various colors. Use flower-shaped clay cutters or freehand sculpting to create petals, leaves, and other floral components.

Assemble Flowers: Layer the clay petals and leaves to create three-dimensional flowers and foliage. Use liquid polymer clay or translucent liquid clay to adhere the components together and to the surface of the vase.

Arrange Flowers: Attach the polymer clay flowers and foliage to the surface of the vase, arranging them in clusters or cascading designs as desired. Use sculpting tools to refine and add detail to the floral arrangements.

Bake: Place the vase on a baking sheet and bake according to the polymer clay manufacturer's instructions. Allow the vase to cool completely before handling.

Finish: Optionally, apply a thin coat of clear varnish or resin to seal and protect the surface of the vase. Display your beautiful polymer clay flower vase proudly!

Polymer Clay Pendant with Faux Gemstone Inlay

Materials Needed:

- Polymer clay (main color and accent colors)
- Rolling pin or pasta machine
- Clay blade or craft knife
- Gemstone or crystal (for reference)
- Liquid polymer clay or translucent liquid clay
- Baking sheet and oven
- Sandpaper (optional)
- Jewelry findings (e.g., jump rings, necklace chain)

Steps:

Prepare the Base: Roll out a sheet of polymer clay to your desired thickness using a rolling pin or pasta machine. Cut out a shape for your pendant using a clay blade or craft knife.

Create Faux Gemstone Inlay: Study the pattern and colors of your chosen gemstone or crystal. Use polymer clay in complementary colors to create a faux gemstone effect. Roll out thin snakes of clay and arrange them on the pendant base to mimic the gemstone pattern.

Smooth and Secure: Use a roller or your fingers to gently press the clay snakes into the base, ensuring they are securely attached. Smooth out any seams or rough edges.

Add Details: Use sculpting tools to add texture and details to the faux gemstone inlay, such as facets or veins.

Bake: Place the pendant on a baking sheet and bake according to the polymer clay manufacturer's instructions. Let it cool completely before handling.

Finish: Sand any rough edges if necessary and polish the pendant with sandpaper for a smooth finish. Optionally, apply a thin coat of clear varnish or resin to enhance the shine. Attach jump rings and a necklace chain to complete the pendant.

Polymer Clay Picture Frame

Materials Needed:

- Polymer clay (various colors)
- Wooden or plastic picture frame
- Rolling pin or pasta machine
- Clay blade or craft knife
- Liquid polymer clay or translucent liquid clay
- Baking sheet and oven
- Sandpaper (optional)

Steps:

Prepare the Frame: Clean the surface of the picture frame and remove any glass or backing. Roll out a sheet of polymer clay to your desired thickness and cover the front surface of the frame with it, smoothing out any air bubbles or wrinkles.

Create Decorative Elements: Roll out sheets of polymer clay in various colors and use clay cutters or freehand sculpting to create decorative elements such as flowers, leaves, or swirls.

Arrange and Attach: Arrange the polymer clay decorative elements on the surface of the frame, adhering them with liquid polymer clay or translucent liquid clay. Experiment with different layouts and designs to create a visually appealing composition.

Bake: Place the picture frame on a baking sheet and bake according to the polymer clay manufacturer's instructions. Let it cool completely before handling.

Finish: Once cooled, sand any rough edges if necessary and apply a thin coat of clear varnish or resin to seal and protect the surface of the frame. Optionally, add a backing and glass to complete the picture frame.

CHAPTER 8
Advanced Projects

Polymer Clay Millefiori Bowl

Materials Needed:

- Polymer clay (various colors)
- Pasta machine or clay roller
- Clay blade or craft knife
- Bowl or mold for shaping
- Liquid polymer clay or translucent liquid clay
- Baking sheet and oven
- Sandpaper (optional)

Steps:

Prepare Clay Canes: Create several intricate polymer clay canes using the millefiori technique. These can include floral patterns, geometric designs, or any other intricate motifs.

Condition and Roll Out Clay: Condition each color of clay and roll them out into thin sheets using a pasta machine or clay roller.

Slice and Arrange Canes: Slice the polymer clay canes into thin discs and arrange them on top of one another in a random or patterned manner.

Layer and Repeat: Layer the slices of clay on top of each other, alternating colors and patterns to create depth and complexity.

Shape the Bowl: Gently press the layered clay onto a bowl or mold to shape it into a bowl form. Smooth out any seams or irregularities with your fingers.

Bake: Place the clay bowl on a baking sheet and bake according to the polymer clay manufacturer's instructions. Let it cool completely before handling.

Finish: Once cooled, sand any rough edges if necessary and polish the surface of the bowl with sandpaper for a smooth finish. Optionally, apply a thin coat of clear varnish or resin to seal and protect the surface.

Polymer Clay Sculpture

Materials Needed:

- Polymer clay (various colors)
- Armature wire or foil
- Sculpting tools (e.g., ball stylus, needle tools)
- Texture tools (e.g., texture sheets, stamps)
- Baking sheet and oven
- Sandpaper (optional)
- Varnish or resin (optional)

Steps:

Plan Your Design: Sketch out your sculpture design and determine the size and proportions of each element.

Create Armature: Build an armature for your sculpture using armature wire or foil. This will provide support and structure for the clay.

Build Basic Shapes: Use polymer clay to create the basic shapes and forms of your sculpture, such as the body, limbs, and facial features. Keep the clay soft and pliable by periodically warming it with your hands.

Refine Details: Use sculpting tools to add details and textures to your sculpture, such as wrinkles, hair, or clothing folds. Take your time to refine the features and ensure they are well-defined.

Bake: Place the sculpture on a baking sheet and bake according to the polymer clay manufacturer's instructions. Let it cool completely before handling.

Finish: Once cooled, sand any rough areas if necessary and apply a coat of varnish or resin to seal and protect the surface. Optionally, paint the sculpture with acrylic paints for added color and detail.

Polymer Clay Filigree Earrings

Materials Needed:

- Polymer clay (multiple colors)
- Jewelry findings (e.g., earring hooks, jump rings)
- Rolling pin or pasta machine
- Clay blade or craft knife
- Needle or toothpick
- Baking sheet and oven
- Liquid polymer clay or translucent liquid clay
- Jewelry pliers

Steps:

Create Filigree Patterns: Roll out thin sheets of polymer clay in various colors using a rolling pin or pasta machine. Use clay blades or craft knives to cut out intricate filigree patterns, such as swirls, scrolls, and floral motifs.

Assemble Earring Components: Cut out matching pairs of filigree pieces for each earring. Layer the pieces to create dimension and interest, using liquid polymer clay or translucent liquid clay to adhere them together.

Add Texture and Details: Use sculpting tools to add texture and fine details to the filigree pieces, such as texture stamps or carving tools. Pay attention to the edges and surfaces to ensure a polished finish.

Create Earring Hooks: Roll out a small piece of clay and shape it into earring hooks or studs. Use jewelry pliers to create loops at the ends for attaching jump rings.

Bake: Place the filigree earring components and earring hooks on a baking sheet and bake according to the polymer clay manufacturer's instructions. Let them cool completely before handling.

Assemble Earrings: Once cooled, attach the filigree components to the earring hooks using jump rings. Ensure that all components are securely attached and properly aligned.

Finish: Sand any rough edges if necessary and apply a gloss varnish or resin to enhance the shine and durability of the earrings. Your stunning polymer clay filigree earrings are now ready to wear or gift!

Polymer Clay Wall Art

Materials Needed:

- Polymer clay (multiple colors)
- Wooden canvas or board
- Rolling pin or pasta machine
- Clay blade or craft knife
- Texture tools (e.g., stamps, texture sheets)

- Baking sheet and oven
- Liquid polymer clay or translucent liquid clay
- Sandpaper (optional)
- Clear varnish or resin (optional)

Steps:

Prepare Canvas: Clean and sand the surface of the wooden canvas or board to create a smooth, even surface for your polymer clay artwork.

Create Polymer Clay Tiles: Roll out thin sheets of polymer clay in various colors using a rolling pin or pasta machine. Use clay blades or craft knives to cut out square or rectangular tiles of uniform size.

Add Texture and Design: Use texture tools such as stamps or texture sheets to add texture and design to the polymer clay tiles. Experiment with different patterns and combinations to create visual interest.

Arrange Tiles: Arrange the polymer clay tiles on the wooden canvas or board to create your desired composition. Play with color placement and tile orientation to achieve the desired effect.

Secure Tiles: Once satisfied with the arrangement, use liquid polymer clay or translucent liquid clay to adhere the polymer clay tiles to the wooden canvas or board. Firmly press each tile to ensure a strong bond.

Bake: Place the polymer clay wall art on a baking sheet and bake according to the polymer clay manufacturer's instructions. Let it cool completely before handling.

Finish: Optionally, sand any rough edges or uneven surfaces with sandpaper for a smooth finish. Apply a coat of clear varnish or resin to seal and protect the surface of the artwork. Your unique polymer clay wall art is now ready to display and admire!

Polymer Clay Kaleidoscope Cane

Materials Needed:

- Polymer clay (multiple colors)
- Rolling pin or pasta machine
- Clay blade or craft knife
- Acrylic rod or cylinder (optional)
- Baking sheet and oven
- Sandpaper (optional)

Steps:

Prepare Clay: Condition each color of polymer clay until soft and pliable.

Create Base: Choose a main color for the base of your kaleidoscope cane. Roll out a thick sheet of this color using a rolling pin or pasta machine.

Build Design: Layer strips of different colored clay on top of the base sheet to create a repeating pattern. Experiment with various colors and shapes to achieve the desired effect.

Reduce and Roll: Once your design is complete, carefully roll up the layered clay sheet into a tight log. Use an acrylic rod or cylinder to ensure even pressure and prevent air bubbles.

Reduce and Stretch: Gently roll and stretch the clay log to elongate it and reduce its diameter. This process helps compress the layers and reveal the intricate pattern inside.

Slice and Reveal: Use a sharp blade or craft knife to slice thin discs from the clay log. Each slice will reveal a unique kaleidoscope pattern. Arrange the slices to form a cohesive design.

Bake: Place the assembled design on a baking sheet and bake according to the polymer clay manufacturer's instructions. Let it cool completely before handling.

Finish: Optionally, sand any rough edges with sandpaper for a smooth finish. Your polymer clay kaleidoscope cane is now ready to be incorporated into various projects, such as beads, pendants, or embellishments.

Polymer Clay Mosaic Wall Art

Materials Needed:

- Polymer clay (multiple colors)
- Wooden board or canvas
- Rolling pin or pasta machine
- Clay blade or craft knife
- Liquid polymer clay or translucent liquid clay
- Baking sheet and oven
- Clear varnish or resin (optional)

Steps:

Prepare Canvas: Clean and sand the surface of the wooden board or canvas to create a smooth, even surface for your mosaic.

Create Mosaic Tiles: Roll out thin sheets of polymer clay in various colors using a rolling pin or pasta machine. Use clay blades or craft knives to cut out small, uniform tiles of different shapes and sizes.

Arrange Tiles: Arrange the polymer clay tiles on the wooden board or canvas to create your desired mosaic pattern. Experiment with color combinations and tile placement to achieve the desired effect.

Secure Tiles: Once satisfied with the arrangement, use liquid polymer clay or translucent liquid clay to adhere the polymer clay tiles to the wooden board or canvas. Firmly press each tile to ensure a strong bond.

Bake: Place the polymer clay mosaic wall art on a baking sheet and bake according to the polymer clay manufacturer's instructions. Let it cool completely before handling.

Finish: Optionally, apply a coat of clear varnish or resin to seal and protect the surface of the mosaic. Your unique polymer clay mosaic wall art is now ready to display and enjoy!

CHAPTER 9
Troubleshooting and Tips

Troubleshooting is an essential part of working with polymer clay, especially when encountering issues during the crafting process.

Cracks or Breakage After Baking:

Possible Causes: Overworking the clay, uneven thickness, insufficient conditioning, or improper baking.

Solutions:

Knead the clay thoroughly to ensure it's soft and pliable before shaping.

Maintain uniform thickness throughout the piece to prevent weak spots.

Avoid sudden temperature changes by preheating the oven and allowing the clay to cool gradually after baking.

Employ an oven thermometer to ensure precise temperature control.

Consider using a support structure or armature for larger or more complex pieces.

Sticky or Soft Clay After Baking:

Possible Causes: Insufficient baking time, incorrect oven temperature, or using old/expired clay.

Solutions:

Bake the clay for the recommended duration at the correct temperature specified by the manufacturer.

Verify your oven temperature's accuracy using an oven thermometer.

If the clay remains soft, rebake it for an additional few minutes to fully cure it. Monitor it closely to avoid burning.

Dust or Debris Embedded in Clay:

Possible Causes: Dust or lint on work surface or tools, or improper storage of clay.

Solutions:

Clean your work surface and tools before starting each project to remove any dust or debris.

Store your clay in a clean, dust-free environment and keep it wrapped in plastic or stored in an airtight container when not in use.

Color Bleeding or Fading:

Possible Causes: Mixing incompatible brands or types of clay, using excessive pressure when blending colors, or improper baking.

Solutions:

Use the same brand and type of clay for all colors in a project to ensure compatibility.

Blend colors gently to avoid smudging or bleeding.

Bake the clay at the correct temperature and duration to preserve color vibrancy.

Surface Imperfections:

Possible Causes: Fingerprints, dust, or texture inconsistencies.

Solutions:

Smooth the surface of the clay with your fingers or a soft brush before baking to remove fingerprints and dust.

Use texture sheets or stamps to add intentional texture and disguise imperfections.

Clay Sticking to Work Surface or Tools:

Possible Causes: Insufficient conditioning, overly warm environment, or using porous work surfaces.

Solutions:

Condition the clay thoroughly to improve its workability and reduce stickiness.

Work in a cooler environment to prevent the clay from becoming too soft.

Use a non-porous work surface such as glass or acrylic, or cover your work surface with parchment paper or wax paper to prevent sticking.

General Tips

Conditioning: Always knead and condition your polymer clay before use to make it soft, pliable, and easy to work with.

If the clay feels too hard, warm it up by kneading it in your hands or passing it through a pasta machine on a low setting.

Clean Workspace: Keep your work surface clean and free of dust, lint, and other debris to prevent imperfections in your clay creations.

Use a lint roller or soft brush to remove any stray particles from your work area and tools before starting a project.

Tools: Use a variety of tools such as clay blades, sculpting tools, texture stamps, and cutters to create different effects and textures in your clay projects.

Keep your tools clean and well-maintained to ensure smooth and precise sculpting.

Baking: Follow the manufacturer's instructions for baking times and temperatures specific to the brand of polymer clay you're using.

Use an oven thermometer to monitor the temperature of your oven and ensure accurate baking.

Safety: Work in a well-ventilated area when conditioning and baking polymer clay to avoid inhaling fumes.

Wash your hands thoroughly after handling polymer clay, especially before eating or touching your face.

Experimentation: Don't be afraid to experiment with different techniques, colors, and designs to discover what works best for you.

Keep a notebook or journal to record your experiments, ideas, and observations for future reference.

Patience: Polymer clay can be forgiving, but it also requires patience and practice to master.

Take your time with each step of the process, from conditioning to sculpting to baking, to achieve the best results.

Storage: Store your polymer clay in a cool, dry place away from direct sunlight to prevent it from drying out or becoming too soft.

Keep different colors of clay separated and organized to avoid color contamination.

Finishing: After baking, sand any rough edges or imperfections with fine-grit sandpaper for a smooth finish.

Apply a clear varnish or resin to seal and protect your finished polymer clay creations and enhance their durability and appearance.

CONCLUSION

Polymer clay offers endless possibilities for creativity and self-expression in jewelry making and various crafts. Throughout this book, we've explored the fundamentals of working with polymer clay, from its origins and essential tools to advanced techniques and troubleshooting tips.

Whether you're a beginner exploring the basics or an experienced crafter pushing the boundaries of your skills, polymer clay provides a versatile medium for endless exploration and innovation. With practice, dedication, and a touch of creativity, you can create unique and personalized jewelry pieces and crafts to cherish and share with others.

As you continue on your polymer clay journey, remember to embrace the process, enjoy the journey, and never hesitate to unleash your imagination. Let your creativity flow freely, and may your polymer clay creations bring joy and inspiration to all who behold them.

www.ingramcontent.com/pod-product-compliance
Lightning Source LLC
Chambersburg PA
CBHW070519290725
30244CB00037B/1322